GOOD MORNING, LORD

Devotions for Men

Lloyd Mattson

BAKER BOOK HOUSE
Grand Rapids, Michigan

Copyright 1979 by
Baker Book House Company
ISBN: 0-8010-6079-6
Second printing, September 1981

Printed in the United States of America

INTRODUCTION

Life is too full for most of us to add frills, but if we look, we can find pockets of idleness even in our busiest days.

Filling these pockets with treasured things is the secret of spiritual serenity for any busy man. This booklet can help you do that.

A small boy wastes no time hunting for his treasures. He has learned they are all about him, and he just pauses to pick them up. Your path will take you by innumerable blessings if you cultivate a searching spirit. Pause now and then, and fill your pockets!

These devotions are one man's thoughts, but the Word is from God. So talk over that Word with the Lord several times a day, and turn it over in your heart. You'll be surprised how often that Word meets some special need in your life.

Search for the way to become the man God wants you to be, and as you become that, you will be everything everyone who cares for you wants you to be.

1

THE ONLY REAL TREASURE

Beloved, let us love one another: for love is of God; and every one that loveth is born of God, and knoweth God.
I John 4:7

Of all the values life can know, which one is supreme? What has genuine, intrinsic worth?

You might include on your list money, fame, power, influence, learning, the arts, property, travel. A case might be made for each one, and all may be used for God's glory. But when you shake down life to its bare essence, you will discover only one object or experience of lasting worth: a friend.

What is the good life? To know the Lord, to enjoy reasonable health, and to own the love of a friend. A caring friend makes even ill health bearable.

Friendship, or Christian love, is the ultimate treasure of life. We have no synonym for *agape*, the biblical word we casually translate love. True friendship is a relationship which defers self-interest to the needs of others, even when others are unworthy or unkind. It is the love of the cross, and it fulfils all other divine laws.

Is such a relationship really possible? Not in man's personal strength; only in Christ. But if you will practice this kind of love when you feel the worst, you will discover the treasure.

2

HARD-LUCK JOHN

He must increase, but I must decrease. John 3:30

Hard work plus God's blessing always brings success. Right? Well, what about John the Baptist?

In a few months John plummeted from fame as the country's leading evangelist to a dungeon and death. You call that success?

Yet Jesus Himself said that no one born of woman was greater than John the Baptist. John did the greatest work any man can do: *He fulfilled God's purpose for his life.* He cared nothing about man's criteria for success.

Most of us expect to slip into comfortable retirement some day, with time for travel, golf, and fishing. We equate success with ease. Dying in prison was not the kind of retirement John looked forward to!

But John had remained true to his prophet's call and faithful to God's special purpose. He had prepared the way for the King, so what did it matter how he slipped from one chapter on earth to the next in eternal life?

3

RITUAL AND RIGHTEOUSNESS

This is pure and undefiled religion in the sight of our God and Father, to visit orphans and widows in their distress, and to keep oneself unstained by the world.
James 1:27, NASB

Between flights a Christian man hurried along a crowded airport concourse one morning, heading for the coffee shop. He came on an elderly woman laden with worn luggage and a shopping bag. Her distress was obvious as she looked this way and that.

Compassion welled up in the man's heart as he strode past. Someone should help that poor woman, he thought. Evidently she was lost.

Then a jolt within halted him as he realized that his urgency was nothing more than a cup of coffee and a newspaper. He turned back, picked up the woman's luggage and met her immediate need.

Together they walked to a distant gate. There was no opportunity for "witnessing," just time to catch a plane to Atlanta.

Years later the man confessed he could not recall what mission carried him to that airport, but he could not forget the ease with which he nearly walked by a person in need. Nor could he forget the smile and the "God bless you!" the woman spoke as they parted. The man wondered if God had sent him all that way to carry an elderly woman's bags.

We measure our faith by our rituals sometimes, whatever those rituals may be. Surely we need orderly worship and personal devotions, and we must be busy about God's work. But we are too busy if we hurriedly pass by the people we are called to serve.

4

TRAINING GROUNDS

Fathers, do not exasperate your children; instead, bring them up in the training and instruction of the Lord. *Eph. 6:4, NIV*

How easy it is to shout from some tower in our adult castle, "No! Don't do that!" A child has never been a father, not even an adult. He can't understand why small mischiefs cause such storms. But since we fathers were once young boys, a good memory can be a powerful aid in raising children.

Don't exasperate your children, wrote Paul. Perhaps we should lay aside our newspapers, get down on the floor, and let our minds trace back as far as they can. No longer will our children have to wait for their dads to come and play.

We need to guide our children in the ways of the church. But more importantly, we need to help them understand that the Lord Jesus hikes and laughs and plays kids' games too. Is not the promise of the Lord as real for children as for adults? Did He not say that He would be with His own always?

Training leads youth into right ways—ways acceptable to God. Sometimes training must include discipline, even spankings, but never punishment when the sole purpose is to vent our anger.

Instruction must surely include the content of the Scriptures. Don't leave the job entirely to the church. Children must be taught in the principles of Christian living. They learn these only through observation.

Paul said in several ways, "As you have seen in me, so do." Dare we say that to our children? We must, for they will model themselves after us, for better or worse.

To train our children in godliness demands that we begin where they are, not exasperating them by expecting what they cannot perform. The hours spent in a child's world grow dearer as the hours recede into history; dearer to the child and far dearer to Dad.

MATCHING PLANS WITH GOD

Then I said, "Here I am—it is written about me in the scroll—I have come to do your will, O God." *Heb. 10:7, NIV*

"God has a wonderful plan for your life" is a phrase you have heard often, but is it true? Does God plot the Christian's course of life?

The very nature of God would argue that this is true, for God is omniscient, omnipotent, and purposeful. His acts are never capricious. But knowing that God has a plan for us, and perceiving what that plan is presents a problem.

Some seem to think we must act as a quarterback waiting for the Lord to send in each play. That's not the way God ordinarily works. Rather, God provides the principles for living in the Word, and He enlightens the brain and spirit to apply those principles to life.

Jesus came to do the will of the Father, and He sends His men into their world to do the same. The route that carried Jesus from the Jordan baptism to Calvary was long and winding, with many small goals along the way. Whatever the big purpose for our lives, faithfulness to each day's task is required. Exciting Christian living grows out of our day-by-day effort to match our plans with God's.

God's plan for most of us will not lead to one great historic climax. It would be a great shame for us to spend our lives waiting for a dramatic moment, and, in the meantime, miss a thousand opportunities to ease a small hurt or share a simple smile.

6

INTO ALL YOUR WORLD

Go ye into all the world, and preach the gospel to every creature. *Mark 16:15*

The Great Commission appears to be a hopeless assignment. The world is so big and the needs are so many, that there seems no way one man can obey Jesus' command.

Although His commission belongs to all Christians, we haven't made much progress in carrying out the commission over the last two thousand years. Only about one-third of the world's people profess any kind of loyalty to Christ.

Perhaps our slow pace in the big world grows out of the failure to evangelize our personal world, the world that begins with each man and reaches out to all who fall under his influence.

To evangelize means to spread the good news of God's love in Christ, then to teach His ways to those who listen. When a life illustrates what God can do for a sinner, people will listen.

Have you evangelized your self world—your mind, body, and spirit? Until you conquer that world for Christ, you won't get very far in other worlds.

Have you evangelized your home world? The first task of every Christian husband is the discipling of his wife and children for Jesus Christ. You can't pass off that assignment to the church!

Have you evangelized the world of your friends and coworkers? A lost person next door or at the next desk is just as lost as a pagan on some distant continent. To profess concern for people far off and hide the good news from people around us is mockery.

THE MARRIAGE MANUAL

Though I speak with the tongues of men and of angels, and have not [love], I am become as sounding brass, or a tinkling symbol. *I Cor. 13:1*

Some of us *talk* a good marriage, but our day-to-day performance leaves much to be desired. We speak the appropriate words, read the right books, lay sound plans, work ourselves weary, and bring home the fruit in ever-larger paychecks. But unless love—genuine Bible love—is present, our deeds are only banging and tinkling.

The need exists to explore the psychology and physiology of marriage, and the marriage manuals do help us, but the grandest of all guides to a happy marriage is found in the Word of God.

Translate I Corinthians 13 into everyday home life. Try the beatitudes of Matthew 5:3–9 on your wife and children. Review that fruit passage, Galatians 5:22–23, in the light of your domestic duties. Climb those eight golden stairs to the abundant life described by Peter (II Peter 1:5–11). Put on Paul's new clothes from Colossians 3:12–15. And return to Solomon's Song. Nature has a wonderful way of caring for psychology and physiology when we properly care for our attitudes.

Remember that the essence of Christian love is meeting the needs of others, no matter how we feel about them at the moment. Self will always be around, reminding us of our hurts and abuses. Deal firmly with self, reminding him that he was crucified with Christ.

Life offers no joy to compare with that of a maturing marriage. The terrifying rate of divorce and shattered happiness indicates that a lot of people, including church people, have missed the secret of joy.

Joy comes through giving of self to fulfil the lives of others, and this joy knows no higher expression than that found between husband and wife when both obey the simple law of love outlined in God's marriage manual.

8

LORD, TEACH US TO PRAY

Ask, and it shall be given you; seek, and ye shall find; knock, and it shall be opened unto you. *Matt. 7:7*

If all the hours we spend studying about prayer were spent in prayer, what miracles would occur! Prayer, like any art, is not mastered through study, but through practice.

And prayer is an art. Prayer renders beauty out of the confusion of our days. Prayer takes the formless mass of our thoughts and intentions and sculpts meaning and delight.

Prayer leads us into good company: first, with the Master who prayed; second, with God's men and women through history who prayed much. All the persons who ever counted for God were given to prayer. Some prayed early, some late. Some lifted language to magnificent heights, others groaned with inarticulate agonies, but all prayed, for God's work demands prayer.

A diamond cutter achieves his work in an instant with one blow of hammer on chisel. Yet before he strikes, he studies the gem long and carefully, blending skill with experience. We tend to see the blow, forgetting the years of reflection and practice on lesser gems. How many blows struck for Jesus failed in their purpose because too little time was given to prayer?

9

PRIME RIB EVERY SUNDAY

Man cannot live on bread alone, but on every word that proceeds out of the mouth of God. *Matt. 4:4, NASB*

Have you observed how carefully we choose our sins? We cry out against the filth and violence of media. We deplore drunkeness and drug abuse. We vote against gambling each time it comes up. But how long has it been since you expressed your disapproval of gluttony?

We would rather not think about it, for our extra rolls of fat lie uncomfortably close. Yet perhaps we should think about it, for fat kills! We tell youth that any practice that violates God's temple (our bodies) is sin. Is there a violator in the crowd?

Jesus' rebuke of Satan was not a vote for poverty. Nor did Jesus disdain good food. He fed the five thousand all they could eat and collected twelve baskets of food that remained. But Jesus refused to turn stones to bread; He refused to exercise His divine power for self-interest.

Paul spoke about a people whose god was their belly. A god is that which commands our devotion above all else. Gluttony is a subtle form of idolatry, and obesity is its judgment.

But we must look beyond bread for the full meaning of Jesus' rebuke. Every appetite God has placed in man has its proper and richest fulfilment in the Spirit-led life. When the sheer pleasure of appetite overpowers a person, joy flees, and judgment follows. When you find yourself condemning the drunkard, grasp that roll of fat just above your belt and squeeze . . . hard.

10

SOUNDING BRASS, TINKLING CYMBALS

Now these three remain: faith, hope and love. But the greatest of these is love. *I Cor. 13:13, NIV*

Too often love is entwined with feelings. The thought Paul sought to convey in I Corinthians 13 goes far beyond those responses that grow out of tender emotions.

Emotions are unreliable and uncontrollable, influenced greatly by how people treat us and by our state of mind. The love Paul described is relational, and holds us accountable regardless of how we may feel at a given moment. This is the crowning gift of the Spirit, the better way. This was the love exemplified by God when He sent His Son (John 3:16).

There is a most wonderful result from this spiritual discipline. When we act out the Christ-life under the most trying circumstances, we discover that our feelings fall in line.

Piety and religious performances do not impress God. Anyone can beat the gong and tinkle the cymbals. God looks for the lilt of love, the resonance of selflessness expressed through Christlike relationships. This is the command of the Spirit for all men of God to all others.

11

WITH YOU ALWAYS

And, lo, I am with you alway, even unto the end of the world. *Matt. 28:20b*

The subject of prophecy stirs excitement in the Christian's heart. Jesus is coming again! We will see Him and share in His eternal kingdom.

Our enthusiasm for Jesus' return must not dim our perception of His current presence. Jesus' reality will not be one wit greater that day when He returns physically than it is today. Only our perception will be altered. The eye of faith tends to blur at times, fogged over by doubt. However, the solution for doubt is at hand: The more we ponder the Word of God, the more clearly we perceive the real presence of Christ in our lives.

When you phone a friend from a distant city, you have no doubt that he is real. But when you call on the same friend in his home, your perception and ability to communicate are strengthened. Jesus' return will be something like that.

Remember that the limitation of spiritual perception is only one-sided. God has no problem knowing you, nor does the truth or strength of His Word depend on your ability to perceive it. You can rely on the truth of Jesus' promise, "Lo, I am with you alway."

When Christ returns, you will see and hear the One you now know by faith. Remember that faith is not a blind conjecture, but a spiritually perceived reality; a different kind of knowing. You can count on His constant presence, for you have His promise.

12

A WALK THROUGH THE ORCHARD

The fruit of the Spirit is love, joy, peace, longsuffering, gentleness, goodness, faith, meekness, temperance; against such there is no law. *Gal. 5:22–23*

You can often tell where a man has been walking by what he carries home. What do you carry when you greet your wife at the door? A briefcase loaded with office chores? A mind still back on the job? That is hardly fair, to her or you!

Bring some fruit of the Spirit home each night this week. On your way home from work, take a walk through the spiritual orchard. You may have to go out of your way a bit to gather fruit, but when you consider the alternatives, the fruit of the Spirit is worth the extra effort.

Recognize any of these: selfishness, dullness of heart, tension, impatience, coarseness, evil, infidelity, boorishness, self-indulgence? Pretty grim diet for those who look to us for strength! And fruit, you know, was planned by God as a means for spreading the seed of the plant.

The prize fruit, of course, is love. Love charges us to live above our feelings, treating others in a Christ-like way no matter how we feel at the moment. We can't reach that fruit unaided, for it grows high. But the Spirit will lift us if we ask Him.

13

ENOUGH FOR GOD'S PURPOSE

There is a lad here, which hath five barley loaves and two small fishes.... *John 6:9*

When we hear the story of Jesus feeding the five thousand, we picture a small boy, crowding in with others, to see this great man, Jesus. It is more likely that the boy was an enterprising young merchant, taking advantage of the crowd to make a nickel selling refreshments.

It really does not matter which he was, for the lesson is the same. Whether our lunch or our merchandise, the Lord can multiply it to be more than enough to fulfil His purpose.

We can only speculate how Andrew came to know about the boy's possession. Perhaps he had heard the boy's shrill voice crying his wares. Or perhaps Andrew was sensitive to young people, and struck up an acquaintance with the boy, learning by chance about the loaves and fishes. Either way, Andrew was the mediator between a boy and the Master.

Perhaps no boy in Galilee ever had such a privilege, or such a story to share with his friends. It was his loaves and fishes Jesus used to feed the crowd that day.

We are honored when God chooses to bless others through us. But we receive double honor when we are alert to the young people around us and lead them to surrender their possessions and persons to Christ.

14

YOU SHALL NOT WANT

The Lord is my shepherd; I shall not want. *Ps. 23:1*

How do we square the heart of the average Christian man with this verse? Let's face it: We *do* want! We want a higher living standard. We want security for old age. We want a better home, a better car, perhaps even a better golf score.

We could squeeze out of the dilemma by declaring that the psalmist meant we would not want for anything necessary to life; we would have enough to survive. But that is risky, for the verse probably means more than that.

The sheep are seen beside still waters, apparently satisfied with their thirst quenched. They are lying down in green pastures, not grazing. The idea seems to be that the Shepherd gives contentment, fulfilment.

However, the Bible instructs Christians to be productive. Since whatever a man does should be done to God's glory, his skills should be used for the maximum benefit of himself and his family, consistent with good stewardship of time.

Think this over: The sheep must be content with the pasture the Shepherd provides, but they must apply themselves to the task of grazing. Whatever the Lord's provision through our gifts and circumstances, we can claim contentment.

Surely it is right to feed well in the pasture God provides and then to rest by His waters of stillness. We need not look beyond to other pastures. To become the best we can in the circumstances of each day delivers us from wanting.

15

THE SECRET PLACE

He that dwelleth in the secret place of the most High shall abide under the shadow of the Almighty. Ps. 91:1

While climbing an ancient spruce one day when I was a boy, I found its spreading boughs would support me. I could lie there secure from discovery and feel part of God's creation, which I had come to love even as a boy. Here was shade in the summer, and shelter from the snow-laden winds in the winter—a perfect secret place for a boy!

But a man needs a secret place too, somewhere to be alone with God. A spruce tree won't do, and usually a private closet is not available. A man's secret place must be found in his heart, present no matter where he might be. Any man who has not found this secret place cannot grow much in Christ.

How good it is to free our minds from the pressing cares of the day, allowing our thoughts to flee to that secret place, where we can pray.

What does one pray about in such moments snatched from the day? Anything and everything! One can chat with the Lord as with a dear companion, speak back the Word to the Author, or give thanks for the many things one enjoys.

This secret place reaches beyond the devotional ritual so useful in the morning. It is a deliberate, disciplined focus of the heart on God whenever the mind is free, a constant awareness of the presence of Jesus. Here we find the shadow of God protecting our spirits from the fiery darts of Satan.

16

WORK OUT YOUR SALVATION?

... work out your own salvation with fear and trembling. *Phil. 2:12*

We know that faith and faith alone effects salvation for a man, but Paul instructed his readers to *work out* their salvation. How do we grasp this paradox?

Remember the jigsaw puzzle that came at Christmas and the late hours you spent huddled over, seeking one elusive piece? It was there, but you had to work it out. And how about that unassembled toy you bought for the youngsters, with instructions to place bolt A in hole B? It was all there; you just had to work it out.

So it is with salvation through faith. Everything we need to live a godly life is available to us, but we have to put the pieces together in everyday experience.

Peter named the seven magnificent segments of a godly life that will lead to guaranteed fruitfulness (II Peter 1:5–8). You will find them familiar; they are old friends from I Corinthians 13 and Galatians 5:22–23. It takes work to root out your natural inclinations and transplant these gracious flowers.

Salvation is free, but it cost God the death of His Son. So although eternal life is a gift, its full realization in life requires demanding work. Far from being a violation of God's grace, this concept is the fulness of grace.

17

HE WALKS ON WATER!

Lord, if it be thou, bid me come unto thee on the water. *Matt. 14:28*

A lot of men forget that there were two who walked on water. Sure, Peter didn't make it all the way, but he went a lot farther than the rest of the twelve.

We remember Peter's failure, and draw lessons from his natural, human fears, yet we forget the courage he displayed by stepping out of the boat in the first place. Most men seem content to sit in the boat and point out the failures of those who dare the unusual, but these are not the ones that change the world.

Peter allowed himself to become vulnerable because of who was out there. Peter tested Jesus' person and power, and Peter made it part way. Even as he failed, Peter learned about Jesus' concern, and His capacity to meet human weakness.

This week, dare to do something unusual for Jesus. The ordinary takes no faith. Sitting securely in the boat accomplishes little. In your home or shop, community or office, what work for God needs attention? Don't be afraid to risk stepping out of the boat, for Jesus will meet you half way!

18

ACT THE MAN

Watch ye, stand fast in the faith, quit ye like men, be strong. *I Cor. 16:13*

Who can become a man of God? As being born male does not by itself assure manliness, neither does being born again by itself make a man a man of God. A man gains the potential for godliness through faith. He earns the marks of godliness through obedience.

Obedience presumes a knowledge of orders, and God has given His orders in the the Word. The man who lives by the Word of God becomes a man of God.

Everything a man does is triggered by some inner force; a thought, an impulse, an instinct. The man who learns to manage those inner forces will manage his life, "for as he thinketh in his heart, so is he" (Prov. 23:7).

Like the computer, output is determined by prior input. When a man programs his thoughts by deep awareness of God's Word, he acts in a godly manner. But this requires more than casual reading; it requires meditating (Ps. 1:3).

Spend time each day in the Word. Reflect on its implications. Talk its ideas back to the Father. The man of God is one bent on the pursuit of godliness, with a desire to share God's love with others.

19

A SAD, WASTED NIGHT?

For it is God which worketh in you both to will and to do of his good pleasure. *Phil. 2:13*

A young minister answered a late-night summons to the home of a dying old man. He did not know the man's family, and the drive was treacherous, as dense fog shrouded the road. The minister could have felt imposed on, for the caller had said the sick man was unconscious.

But the pastor came quickly, passed through an old-fashioned living room crowded with mourning neighbors, and knelt by the bed in a room just off the parlor. Taking the emaciated hand of the nearly dead man, the minister spoke the promises of Christ and prayed. There was no evidence that the man heard, and later that night he died.

A wasted night? Why hadn't the family called before the man lost consciousness? Death-bed evangelism seemed uncertain at best to the minister as he thought now and then about that pensive visit.

A few years later another phone call came, from a young mother deeply desiring to know the Lord. Her conversion was clear and joyous. The minister was curious, for, to the best of his memory, he had never met this person. He asked why she had called for him.

"You remember a night several years ago when you came to a farm home to pray with an old man who was dying? I was one of those who sat in the living room. You seemed to care for that man, though I knew you had never met him. I felt you would care for me, too."

From this experience, the young minister discovered a truth that never left him. God does not insist that we see results, only that we be faithful. A disappointment, a puzzling failure, a dreadful inconvenience—but who knows what God has in mind for the future? Some of God's best work happens when we least expect it.

20

THE WHATSOEVER GOSPEL

... Whatsoever ye do, do all to the glory of God.
I Cor. 10:31

We talk much about the *whosoever* gospel, the good news for all people. We talk less about the *whatsoever* gospel, the good news that our total life is rich in spiritual potential.

Ask any group to enumerate the things that most please God. You will get a list of religious performances such as prayer, Bible study, witnessing, church attendance, public service for God.

Calculate how much time the typical Christian man devotes to such activity. If you can come up with a tithe of the week, you're doing remarkably well! What then of the rest of the week?

Christ put an end to the old covenant and left us not a religion to take its place, but a way of life—a pattern for spiritual awareness to invade every moment and deed.

The "reasonable service" of Romans 12:1 is really spiritual worship, the closest term we have describing the religion of the Christian. Paul said this involves presenting our bodies as living sacrifices.

The Christian including his every act, thought, and intention, is totally God's. Spiritual disciplines are necessary for growth, and Christians need the fellowship of the body of Christ. But the gospel on Sunday will never reach its full potential until we discover the whatsoever gospel of all week.

21

IN THE SPIRIT
ON THE LORD'S DAY

I was in the Spirit on the Lord's day, and heard behind me a great voice, as of a trumpet. *Rev. 1:10*

Shallow praying produces shallow living. Our hurried age leaves little time for the pursuit of God in quiet depth, and we are the worse for it. Without deliberate effort we will never share John's experience of being in the Spirit on the Lord's day and hearing from heaven. Even our worship services are so fully scheduled that there is little time for reflection.

What would we learn if we kept count of our hours for a week? What interests would consume the bulk of our time? Of course we must spend time commuting, working, eating, and sleeping, but what of the hours that remain?

How would time spent reading, watching television, or working at our hobbies compare with those devoted to spiritual disciplines? We need to make a private quiet time to pray and read our Bibles. Even birdwatchers find their best specimens on predawn walks and trout fishermen do best in the solitude of wooded streams.

Does God find a place among our most compelling interests? Measured by the hours we spend, how would we rate the importance of our Christian faith? Granted that we belong full-time to God, how many hours each week belong exclusively to Him?

John was in the Spirit on the Lord's day and he saw a new vision. It may work for us too!

A WOUNDED FLOWER

And we know that all things work together for good to
them that love God, to them who are the called according to his purpose. *Rom. 8:28*

Looking back, you can probably find some failure
or hurt you can't possibly believe will ever come to
any good purpose in your life. Is Romans 8:28 true?

I learned something about its truth from a tiny,
lavender daisy-like flower at the crest of Twisp Pass
high in the Cascades. I no longer question the potential for good in any experience of life, even my failures and hurts.

Sitting on a huge boulder alongside a trail, I pon-
dered the valley far below, tracing the white thread
of a tumbling stream as it wound among firs. I was
weary, sore of foot, disgruntled, and angry at the
man whose pack I carried. My horse had gone by,
joined to the small herd of pack animals, due to
another man's miscalculations. It was, I determined,
a rotten day.

Then I saw the flower, growing from a crevice in
my boulder couch. All around me were myriads of
the tiny blooms, so I dared pluck this one, for it
seemed to have a beauty somehow different than its
sisters.

Close examination revealed that my flower displayed a deep crimson mark near its golden eye, a
mark I could detect in no other flower. Curiosity
drove away my petty irritations, and I sought the
cause for this distinctive loveliness.

I solved the riddle. One tiny petal lay curled

against the eye, its lavender pressed into a crimson curl. Sometime in its brief past, a calamity overtook my flower, wounding one of its rays. In the wounding, the petal curled, adding a crimson beauty mark.

Do you suppose God smote a tiny flower, knowing that soon a weary pilgrim would need refreshing?

That couldn't be, could it?

23

HUSBANDS LOVE YOUR WIVES

Whoso findeth a wife findeth a good thing. *Prov. 18:22*

Most of us succeed in persuading some girl to marry us. Some try but fail. A few choose not to marry, seeking life goals that are best accomplished outside of marriage. Generally it is thought, however, that man functions best with a mate.

Those of us so blessed that we enjoy the love of a wife, can survive almost any trial outside the home. We understand why God chose the image of marriage for Christ and the church.

The first duty of every Christian husband is the spiritual and physical enrichment of his wife. No man who leaves his wife lonely and unfulfilled, can do a good work for God.

We tend to dwell on one sentence in Paul's writings: "Wives, submit yourselves unto your own husbands, as unto the Lord" (Eph. 5:22).

But Paul lays a more difficult charge on men when he writes, "Husbands, love your wives, even as Christ loved the church, and gave himself for it" (Eph. 5:25). Submission places responsibility on another, but love demands initiatives. No wife will find difficulty in submitting to a husband who spends his life being Christlike.

No man has a right to demand obedience to the Scriptures on the part of his wife, if he has not first obeyed this command to love. The awesome measure of a husband's love for his wife is to be as Christ's love for the church. The price of that love was the cross.

HOW DO YOU FEEL ABOUT SNAKES?

As Moses lifted up the serpent in the wilderness, even so must the Son of man be lifted up: That whosoever believeth in him should not perish, but have eternal life. *John 3:14–15*

No other creature stirs such revulsion and fear as the lowly serpent. That most snakes are harmless and helpful makes no difference; the impulse persists to kill every snake in sight.

We trace this people-snake enmity back to the garden, where Satan, as a serpent, beguiled Eve, bringing the curse and fixing that hatred between woman and snake. This is a curious and mysterious bit of history.

But the main issue is not human kind's terror of snakes; it is the continuing enmity between the seed of the serpent and the seed of the woman. Many see this as the Bible's first promise of a Redeemer, one who would crush the head of the serpent.

The Redeemer's power over the serpent falls into graphic perspective in the story of the fiery serpents in Moses' day (Num. 21:6). When the grumbling Israelites confessed their sin and cried for deliverance, God instructed Moses to cast a bronze serpent and suspend it on a pole. God promised that all who were bitten by the deadly snakes had only to look to the brazen serpent and the poison would not kill them.

Here in symbol was God's fulfillment of all the promises of a Savior. The cause of death became the source of life as men looked to the serpent and lived. He who knew no sin was made to be sin, and there, suspended high over history, Jesus bore the guilt of sin that man might live. All who look are freed from death's sting.

THE SKY WATCH

Ye men of Galilee, why stand ye gazing up into heaven? *Acts 1:11*

"Keep looking up!" is a cheery motto! With all the misery and gloom in our world, the upward look makes sense. Why, then, did those two white-clad strangers ask the question that seems tinged with rebuke?

There are three possible reasons. For one thing, Jesus had issued an order that could not be obeyed there on the Mount of Olives. Also, He had given a promise that could not be fulfilled until the men got back to Jerusalem. Finally, Jesus' return was certain; no amount of sky watching would affect it one way or another.

Enthusiasm for prophecy is commendable and spiritually enriching, but it is possible to make the Second Coming a hobby that inhibits obedience to God's day-by-day assignments.

Yet there is a good reason to look upward, for our citizenship and our investments are in heaven. The only enduring values possible for the Christian man relate to eternity.

The worth of our heavenly investments will not be measured by how accurately we perceive prophetic detail; but by how faithfully we fulfil our earthly commissions. It is good to know Christ will return, and it is stimulating to keep track of the signs of His coming, but our assignments cannot be fulfilled out on Mount Olivet. We must get back to Jerusalem, receive the promise, and get on with today's task for the coming King.

HE WAS A FOOL

Then Jacob gave Esau bread and pottage of lentils; and he did eat and drink, and rose up, and went his way; thus Esau despised his birthright. *Gen. 25:34*

There was a man with a beautiful wife, two little girls, and a thriving business who worked with an attractive woman on the church social committee. They prayed together, worked hard together, and he kindly drove her home after committee meetings. He was a fool.

There was a minister who counseled discouraged women in his study. He prayed with them, cared for them, and broke the heart of his wife. The minister is looking for a job. He was a fool.

Every man is a fool who thinks he is above temptation. He is thrice a fool when he enters mild flirtations. There are no extenuating circumstances, no winds of fate that sweep two innocent people into sudden passion, but there are fools who trade their birthrights for a bowl of pottage.

It is not weakness to admit temptation is stronger than virtue. Human sexuality is both man's greatest source for joy, and his greatest enemy. Affairs don't just happen; they are carefully plotted, however far back in our minds we thrust the plotting. The man who seeks a harlot is more honorable than the Christian who compromises his spiritual birthright to the destruction of home and church.

God said "Thou shalt not commit adultery." But even though God will forgive, and a wife and church will forgive, things can never be the same again. And the wreckage strewn on the coasts of God's kingdom because of selfish fools can never be fully repaired.

THE MEMORY PORTFOLIO

Remember now thy Creator in the days of thy youth, while the evil days come not, nor the years draw nigh, when thou shalt say, I have no pleasure in them. *Eccles. 12:1*

One day I visited an old man who lived alone in a large, expensive home. He was rich and lonely. On the fireplace mantle were neat rows of photos, and as we chatted I learned that all the man had left were pictures—no memories.

This man was learning that life is the sum of its friends and its memories, and memory collecting can be put off too long. He had paid a dear price for success.

The family represented by those photos had grown up and gone away before he knew it, and he hadn't counted on his wife dying so young. They had planned to do so much when he got the business in shape. The business was in fine shape now and money was rolling in, but the memory collecting years were over.

Don't let success rob you of the real wealth of old age. Sometimes a cut in pay and more time with Dad is the best income a family can know. Many men who took an extra job to pay for a child's education discovered they had no child when college years came. Children need a dad, not a bank account.

While you are busy planning for retirement, don't forget your investment in memories. Stocks and bonds are a mocking substitute for adventures to remember. Build your memory portfolio carefully.

28

WHOSE SON ARE YOU?

Whose son are you, young man? *I Sam. 17:58, NASB*

Saul asked David that question on a notable day. Certain rewards had been promised to the family of anyone who would destroy the giant Goliath, and Saul was fulfilling his promise.

Saul's question recognized a father's role in shaping character that dared to fight a giant. The mightiest warriors in Saul's army trembled in fear, while a puny teenager whirled his sling.

Jesse had a right to be proud that day, but the seeds of David's victory had been planted long before. Someone had taught the boy useful skills and provided challenging experiences. In fact, David had already killed lions and bears. And someone had also introduced David to the Lord. Had it been the aging father?

When the challenge came, David was ready. His war cry was, "The battle is the Lord's!" You can be certain he prayed, but it was practice that guided the stone, and confidence that committed a youth to the battle. How will our young people fare when they face their Goliaths?

The only hope for victory lies in the home, where mothers and fathers share the awesome task of building Christian character. Saul saw the strength of a father in a son like David. Ultimately our children must make their own choices, but we parents must present God's options clearly, lovingly, and firmly.

29

THE VOICE OF MY BELOVED

The voice of my beloved! behold, he cometh leaping
upon the mountains, skipping upon the hills. *Song of
Sol. 2:8*

Before centuries of God's people heard Solomon's
allegory of God's love for His own, a woman found
joy in her love poem from a king, and she responded
in kind.

What a joyous exercise of devotion and love it
would be for husband and wife to read to each other
these love poems. How soon we allow romance to
fade from marriage, to be replaced with the weary
tedium of housekeeping, job tending, and child-
rearing. Without regular reminders of love, life cannot escape tedium.

Little surprises such as a flower, a small gift, an
I-love-you card, mean so much when they are given
for no special occasion. Too busy for that? When
time for love is crowded out, you are too busy. All
that your busyness is gaining will be lost when you
look back someday.

Marriages grow weary because so much that we
call love is merely self-seeking. How difficult it is to
put aside our personal moods to accommodate the
needs of another. How readily we allow our wife and
family to blend with the furniture and wallpaper as
pleasant conveniences.

The presence of the Song of Solomon in the Bible
assures us of the importance of romantic love in life,
and should encourage us to communicate openly
and tenderly our intimate thoughts to our God-given

mate. What feelings are awakened when your wife hears your step approaching after work? Does she fear your mood? When you feel least like leaping and skipping, then you must leap. The other days will care for themselves.

Should a wife ever wait anxiously for the step of her husband, to know if that step will be heavy or light? Should fear or uncertainty ever mar the anticipation of a wife? Think carefully how your voice will sound to the one you call beloved. Plan soon to read together the Song of Solomon, God's gift to man and wife.

30

HOW ARE YOUR MUSCLES TODAY

Physical exercise has some value, but spiritual exercise is valuable in every way, because it promises life both for the present and for the future. *I Tim. 4:8, TEV*

You have seen ads in magazines that show Mr. Atlas' marvelous muscles and promise that you too almost miraculously can turn from a ninety-seven pound weakling into the strongest man on the beach.

Perhaps you quietly sent for the secrets, only to learn that there was a considerable price involved, more than you could pay. There is always a price for strength, whether it be physical, intellectual, or spiritual.

Many of us could use some exercise, for both mind and body. But most of us are not likely to pay the price. There are many men who jog every day in the predawn dusk, following a circuit of several miles. Rain or sleet, heat or cold, they jog their lonely route. Other men will not sleep until they have read their allotted chapters in a rigorous mind-improvement plan.

And there are a few men, who pay heed to their souls, who set aside time to pray and read the Word. They read and pray alone, for the price they pay is too dear for most men.

But is praying and reading the Bible necessary? No. Neither is jogging or studying. Casual Christian fellowship, prayer meetings, Bible classes, and sermons provide a basic diet. After all, no one measures the spiritual biceps or tests the I.Q. of the soul. You can get along without spiritual discipline. Many do.

Yet, now and then you hunger for more than you know, and wish you were not so flabby of soul. You can change all that if you will give your spirit disciplined, careful exercise. The rewards will be truly exhilarating!

ASAPH'S PROBLEM

When I thought to know this, it was too painful for me;
until I went into the sanctuary of God; then I under-
stood their end. *Ps. 73:16–17*

Asaph had a problem that many of us face now and
then: What is the use of living honestly? Look how
the crooks prosper!

Government corruption, petty thievery, misrepre-
sentation and false pricing, shady deals—whatever
the form of cheating, most crooks seem to get by.
They grow fat and rich, while the honest man strug-
gles.

Almost anyone can cheat and escape detection.
The ability to remain honest when the act of cheating
without getting caught is possible, is a measure of
our faith. Foolish are Christians who compromise for
petty thefts. Thieves always pay their dues, sooner or
later.

When Asaph entered the sanctuary he learned the
value of personal integrity, for he saw the end of the
wicked. Asaph's envy dissolved in God's meeting
place.

All men must enter a meeting place with God
someday. The man of God will enter the sanctuary
where the Savior stands with the scars of the cross
still present in His outstretched hands, and the treasures of life in Christ Jesus will be all about him.

But the smirking thief, petty or grand, will enter a
hall of judgment clad in rags. The Judge will pro-
nounce an irrevocable sentence of torture.

32

TURN ON THE POWER!

For I am not ashamed of the gospel of Christ: for it is the power of God unto salvation to every one that believeth. *Rom. 1:16a*

A backwards woodsman once received a chain saw for Christmas. A few weeks later he returned the gift, explaining that he could accomplish more work with his old buck saw. Puzzled, the donor pulled the starter cord to learn what was wrong. The woodsman jumped with amazement. "What's that noise?"

Sometimes we Christians are like that. We struggle to make Christianity work without turning on the Power. Attempting God's work without God's power is futile. If that were possible, Christ need not have died.

Man's best benevolent, sacrificial efforts cannot save one lost sinner nor ease one spiritual burden. Yet we keep trying. If only we can find the right system or combination of attractive programs, then we can move people for God. But all we get are the benefits of systems and programs. God through His prophet Zechariah said that it is not by human might or power that His work is accomplished, but "by my Spirit" (Zech. 4:6).

We must carry out God's work by the leading of His Spirit in humility and love and with fear and trembling, for His work is eternal.

GOD'S FINAL WORD

In the beginning was the Word, and the Word was with God, and the Word was God. *John 1:1*

The Bible declares unequivocally that Jesus is God. If you believe the Bible, you must believe in the absolute deity of Jesus. If Jesus is less than God, then the Bible tells a lie, and we are without a sure word from heaven.

But since we have found the Bible to be true, and are assured that Jesus was God become man, we can face life with a perspective different from that of most persons. Christians know and understand things that non-Christians can't even imagine.

The writer to the Hebrews said that God spoke in times past through the prophets to the fathers, speaking in bits and pieces. But in recent days, God had spoken through His Son, and when the Son had completed His redemptive work, He sat down at the right hand of His Father (Heb. 1:1–3).

Jesus not only spoke God's gracious words to man but Jesus was also God's Word. God spoke in the person of His Son, and Jesus is God's final word to man.

Man resists this idea, clinging to some fragment of human wisdom and worth. To acknowledge Jesus as true God puts an end to human judgment and demands submission.

This is more than most men's pride can bear, thus many turn away from salvation. To receive the gift of life in Christ Jesus demands surrender to His lordship.

THE MADMAN OF THE TOMBS

Then they went out to see what was done; and came to Jesus, and found the man, out of whom the devils were departed, sitting at the feet of Jesus, clothed, and in his right mind: and they were afraid. *Luke 8:35*

What a picture of spiritual deliverance this is! Shortly before, this same man had run screaming among the cave tombs of the hillside. He tore the clothes from his body with unblushing abandon. His mind was enslaved to demons. He was restless, shameless, and mindless. Sound familiar?

The sounds of our world tell the restlessness of people. We hear the screams of sirens, the throb and howl of music, the sobs of battered women and children, the screech of tires and death; it is almost impossible to find a quiet place on the face of this restless earth.

Shame is a forgotten word. Moral rot has eaten away at human-kind, leaving the world naked and ugly. As a result of immorality, our hospitals are filled with the sick of mind—blown minds, broken minds.

The madman of the Gadarene tombs is the picture of our world today. For the world, as for him, one cure exists. He had the good sense to run to Jesus.

The people begged Jesus to leave the area, for they preferred their pigs to deliverance. He left, but He left behind one who knew God's power. From his posture of peace at the feet of Jesus, the freed man returned to his town. Even those who lamented the loss of their pigs could not help but notice the change.

BEACH YOUR BOATS

And when they had brought their ships to land, they forsook all, and followed him. *Luke 5:11*

One has to wonder what passed through the minds of the four fishermen as they tugged their boats from the water and walked off with Jesus. They could not imagine what adventures lay ahead, for them or for the Master.

Following Christ meant a change in vocation for the fishermen. For most of us, it means something else. The Lord does not call all men into religious vocations, which we call "full-time service," but we who stay at our jobs have boats to beach as well.

Peter and his crew could have protested and offered to join the reserves, serving only on weekends. Quite a few Christian men try that, but Jesus said, "follow me," and He works every day. The men had to beach their boats.

While your sphere of service differs from those assigned to church-related vocations, your responsibilities are the same. What gets in your way as you follow God's direction? Every hindrance must be abandoned to gain the adventures of discipleship.

Too costly, you say? You are forgetting that great catch of fish Jesus provided just before He called the fishermen from their boats. Did the Twelve ever suffer want?

The fishermen went off for greater game than they had sought in their trade. You will wonder how you could have ever been so attached to whatever it is you must put away to follow the Master.

Beach your boat and follow!

LIVING BY FAITH

O the depth of the riches both of the wisdom and knowledge of God! how unsearchable are his judgments, and his ways past finding out! *Rom. 11:33*

Philosophy and theology will never fully satisfy men's hearts. But faith accepts God as He is with all His inexplicable paradoxes. Faith does not demand empirical evidence, though faith recognizes satisfying proofs. We cannot package God through faith and present Him to the unbelieving world in convincing manner as one would an archaeological artifact, saying, "There, you see?"

When we accept this, many frustrations become manageable. How can reasonable men reject the gospel? Reason is not the faculty that grasps spiritual truth, faith is. Without that Spirit-born stirring, that unrest of soul, man will not listen to God. And it is God who must be heard, not our voices.

Man convinced against his will remains unconvinced. Our best arguments may make an impact, but man has a facility for persisting in unbelief. The best we can do is present Jesus' teachings clearly and lovingly, then live at peace. Jesus Himself failed to persuade His own countrymen, though He worked miracle after miracle before them.

As God's servant, you can represent Him where He chooses to send you, and you can become part of His master plan to win from among lost mankind those who will exercise the gift of faith.

THE EYES OF THE SPIRIT

... Lord, I believe; help thou mine unbelief. *Mark 9:24*

We all share the problem of the man who, in urgency for the life of his son, cried out this phrase.

How is this possible? Because we all see through two pairs of eyes: the eyes of the body and the eyes of the spirit. Our marvelous physical eyes receive light which the brain interprets. We see form, texture, color, motion; and seeing is believing. But the spiritual eye relies on other data, and the mind has trouble with this.

The writer to the Hebrews said that faith is substance and evidence, and so it is; but we must possess the proper equipment for faith to perceive its subjects. There is little wonder that men who don't know God scoff at the reality of faith: they are not equipped to see. Faith is a gift from God, and its validity does not depend on our ability to exercise it perfectly or convince others of its reality.

We see distortions as though through a mirror, Paul said. Someday the distortions will clear, and we will see Christ face to face. Meanwhile, belief and unbelief will war in our hearts. Read God's Word and cast your reliance on His promises. Light from the Word will brighten your vision.

38

SPEAK UP!

But speak the things which become sound doctrine.
Titus 2:1

When next you are in the company of Christian friends, listen. What do you hear? Speech is a fairly accurate barometer of the soul. Does our talking reflect the fulness of God's love within?

As he warmed himself by the fire the night before Christ's crucifixion Peter's accent betrayed him as one of Jesus' followers. With curses Peter attempted to disclaim any part with Jesus. People know what we are by our speech.

James says much about the tongue, and his writing merits frequent review. We must give an account someday for every idle word we speak. That is frightening!

The gift of speech may be our most abused faculty. How carelessly we talk, using poor diction, a lazy vocabulary, and hastily formed ideas. We prattle inanely and seldom listen. What topics occupy your conversation when you chat with friends?

Speech reflects the state of our hearts. When anger arises, try speaking softly. See what happens! Is there someone against whom you feel badly? Say something sincerely nice to him; you will be amazed how feelings change. Must you speak reprovingly to someone? Speak the truth in love, and your reproof will gain its end much more readily.

Speak up for God. Tell what He means to you. Match your readiness to talk about the weather and taxes with a confident word for Christ. If you had but one final sentence to utter, what would it be?

UNHINDERED PRAYERS

Husbands, dwell with them according to knowledge, giving honor unto the wife as unto the weaker vessel, and as being heirs together of the grace of life; that your prayers be not hindered. *I Peter 3:7*

How a man treats his wife controls the effectiveness of his prayers. You may be a shining light in church, but unless there is a love glow at home, your praying cannot reach far.

In Christ there is no male or female (Gal. 3:28). The leadership of the husband is not that of a lord over a slave, but of a lover over a beloved one. The Bible presents a mutuality of concern; man for woman and woman for man, with the greater burden on the man.

That mysterious oneness of husband and wife reaches beyond their immediate moments. They are heirs together of the grace of life—all joys and sorrows, hopes and uncertainties. Children reflect what mother and father are together, more than what they are individually, passing on strengths and weaknesses in turn to their children. The grace of life reaches down to future generations.

When daily prayer forms an essential part of home life, immediate benefits are gained. Anticipating prayer renders us less likely to yield to our selfish impulses. Sharing prayer softens the spirit to say, "I'm sorry," when that is needful. Praying about circumstances of potential tension puts the problem in a spiritual perspective and prepares the heart to make appropriate decisions.

God will grant a gracious, joyous life to those who walk together with Him.

UNFAILING TRAINING

Train up a child in the way he should go: and when he is old, he will not depart from it. *Prov. 22:6*

How many fathers have read this proverb through tears and asked what went wrong? These fathers forget a vital part of the promise: "*when he is old, he will not depart from it.*" It is the nature of people that childhood impressions may take some years to rise to the top.

But a deeper problem must be considered as we train our children in the way. What constitutes effective training? Sadly, most children recruited to Sunday school in early childhood are lost to the church before they reach their midteens. When neither parent attends church, almost all youngsters drop out. When both parents faithfully share in church life, most of their children continue as well. Example continues to be the only effective training tool available to us as fathers.

What you are, your children will likely become—sooner or later. We must not ignore the powerful negative influences competing for our children's loyalties. Do you monitor the television in your home? Do you know what the schools are teaching? Our children spend more waking hours with television and school than they do with us.

The dominant influence on your children as they reach adolescence will be their friends. They will cause your children to break your heart if their lifestyle is contrary to your wishes. But when you work to create the right kind of friendships for your children, those friends will become your most powerful allies.

Lead your children to Christ. Live Christ honestly before them. Work and pray mightily that your children may form the right friendships. In other words, train your children in the way they should go.

PEACE, BROTHER

Now the Lord of peace himself give you peace always
by all means. The Lord be with you all. *II Thess. 3:16*

How is your supply of peace today? Running low?
Renewal is as close as a whisper. Isaiah promised
perfect peace from the Lord to those who fixed their
minds on Him. Jesus spoke peace to the sea and to
His troubled disciples. Paul echoed the promise of
peace in his benediction to the Thessalonian Christians, and he identified the source of peace as the
presence of Christ in life.

Peace belongs to all who enjoy the presence of
Jesus in their lives. Consider what robbed you of
peace lately. Was it the assertion of self over faith for
a time? Was money at stake? Was your child in moral
or physical danger? Did temptation get the best of
you? And did you forget for a time Who walks beside
you?

The restoration of peace is but a whisper away.
You never need to shout to catch Jesus' attention.
When peace next takes leave of you, talk it over
boldly with the Lord. You will be pleased with the
results.

When you are under stress, consider what is the
worst that could happen. Is not the Lord more than
sufficient for even that need? Fix Isaiah's promise
and Paul's benediction in mind as your amulet
against fear. "Thou wilt keep him in perfect peace,
whose mind is stayed upon thee: because he trusteth
in thee" (Isa. 26:3).

42

WITNESS AND WITHNESS

And he ordained twelve, that they should be with him, and that he might send them forth to preach. *Mark 3:14*

Jesus chose twelve that they might be *with* Him, and that He might send them forth. Fellowship precedes service, and without fellowship, service has no power.

Prayer must not become mere duty, or an exercise in getting. Prayer should be intimate communion, fellowship with God. We do not summon God, or command His attention. We come as guests, invited into His presence. Whatever the pleasure He takes in our company, it is to bless and renew our spirits.

Like we welcome a son or daughter calling home, a former student dropping by, or a long-time friend knocking at the door; somehow God finds pleasure in our prayers.

Jesus' disciples were not really of much use to Him. They argued among themselves, sought special privileges, and finally betrayed, denied, and forsook Him. Yet Jesus loved them! And so He loves us.

As you ponder our text, think how you felt those times when someone said, "I'm sorry I didn't call; I really *meant* to." Take time today and every day to visit with the Lord. He wants you to be with Him, and certain blessings will follow as He sends you forth.

43

ALL THESE THINGS

Seek ye first the kingdom of God, and his righteousness; and all these things shall be added unto you.
Matt. 6:33

Three times the Lord repeated the words, "all these things," in a brief passage of His magnificent sermon. Don't be anxious over things, He said.

But when you have a family to feed, clothe, and house; retirement to save for; and college educations for your children to pay for, isn't a little worry almost necessary? Jesus never taught that we should ignore parental responsibility.

Awareness and planning have nothing to do with that spiritually debilitating anxiety Jesus warned against. Consider the birds, He said. Did you ever see a robin perched on a limb, mouth open, waiting for a worm from heaven? Robins constantly seek food for themselves and their young. Birds are busy creatures, but they do sing a lot.

Consider the flowers, Jesus said. Watch a new shoot push its way through the earth, reaching for light and air. Pluck a dandelion and note how its roots dig deeply into the soil in search of nutrients and moisture. Flowers, like birds, expend energy almost constantly to fulfill the natural laws the Creator determined for their survival.

No Christian man worth his salt would idle away his time, content to live off the work of others. God has provided for all His creatures, including man, an environment that contains all that is needful. But we must work for it. As we work, we should sing praises to God who gave us life and the capacity to work.

GOD IS ABLE

Now unto him that is able to keep you from falling, and to present you faultless before the presence of his glory with exceeding joy, to the only wise God our Saviour, be glory, and majesty, dominion and power, both now and ever. Amen. *Jude 24*

Faith rests on the knowledge that God is able. The essence of faith is that trustful self-surrender to God that accepts all of His promises as truth.

It is one thing to say this, but quite another to practice it. Let's presume a choice was forced on us: our faith or a sudden, tax-free million dollars. Since the possibility is safely remote, we affirm we would choose our faith, but how do we know?

One index can be found in the little choices we make, our insignificant compromises that none but us see—compromises in thought, mild compromises of integrity or truth; our expense account, or pirated supplies from the plant.

Does God notice such things? The bigger question is this, does our gain merit petty, questionable practice? If a box of paper clips from central supply slips harmlessly home, might not a million dollars tempt us too?

God is able to keep us from falling, to bring us into His presence faultless with full joy, but we need to practice on the little things.

You can be certain the acrobat practices with his catcher many hours before climbing to the high trapeeze and putting away the net. Practice in simple routines gives him confidence for the high triple somersault. You can be sure God will never miss, but half of success rests with you.

45

WHAT TIME IS IT, GRANDPA?

Teach us to order our days rightly, that we may enter the gate of wisdom. *Ps. 90:12, NEB*

I can still hear that voice calling up the stairs to my study. "What time is it, Grandpa?" That was the first time anyone ever called me "Grandpa!"

To me, *Grandpa* was my father, or my grandfather. Suddenly it seemed that my son was grown, and his son had been born, and called up the stairs, "Grandpa, what time is it?"

The strange feeling stayed with me for days. It was later than I had realized. The supply of days that had seemed so endless was darting off this way and that, with no proper leave taking. Years that had followed a leisurely pace suddenly rushed on, accelerated by next year's calendar already filling. Life picks up speed fast on the downhill side!

A sense of frustration that time would run out before half the needful work was done pressed me for weeks. Then one morning sanity and peace returned. From somewhere came a thought: When you have eternal life, what's the hurry?

Calm takes over when you discover that the Christian's life is inviolate until God's purpose is fulfilled. That is neither fatalism nor a spiritualized shunning of responsibility. In a hurry-up world, this philosophy offers the only peaceful course.

What time is it? Time enough for all God asks—time for Him and others.

IF YOU WOULD TEACH

You heard my teaching in the presence of many witnesses; put that teaching into the charge of men you can trust, such men as will be competent to teach others. *II Tim. 2:2, NEB*

We're all teachers of one sort or another. Someone is modeling themselves after us, or accepting as truth what we say. That has frightening implications for the committed Christian man.

But we can't escape it. Teaching is the essential element in Christian discipleship. The root idea behind disciple is *learner*, and a learner must have a teacher.

The most common title used when addressing Jesus was Master, or Teacher. He was always teaching whether to a crowd of thousands, a dozen men, or one woman. The climax of Jesus' three-part Great Commission was, "Teaching them to observe whatsoever things I have commanded you." So we must be teachers if we are to fulfill Christ's purpose.

What makes teaching effective? Reflect for a moment on your school days. Probably the subject matter has blended into a pastel landscape with too much already beyond the horizon! But you recall vividly certain teachers and certain moments. You remember teachers you liked most and least. And you remember moments of great elation and gloom.

Paul wrote, "Speaking the truth in love . . ." (Eph. 4:15). Where love prevails, teaching has an excellent chance for success. And should the student forget the lesson, he will remember the teacher.

THE HARD PLACE

In all these things we are more than conquerors through him that loved us. *Rom. 8:37*

A mountain hiker soon learns that the trail is best discerned from a summit looking back. Contemplating a climb from the valley does not fully reveal the joys and trials ahead. But when one gains the heights and sees where he has come, he is glad he didn't know it all beforehand.

God rarely lays out His full plan for a man many years in advance. Perhaps you're quite amazed to be where you presently find yourself, considering your past dreams and plans. It's possible you're disappointed just now. Tragedy may have cast its shadow over your path. Keep plodding on. An uphill trail always leads to a summit, and you'll catch your wind and perhaps see the need for the steep place and hard crossing you wonder at now.

Moses spent forty years in the desert. Joseph, Daniel, and Paul spent weary years in jail. Job lost everything except his life. But better days lay ahead for all of them, and better days await you.

The joy of any worthy hike is not the destination, but the journey. To press on, head down, just to get there makes little sense. It is what you experience along the trail that will live in your memory once you are back home.

Dare to taste life as you go, the bitter and sour moments, too. None know the comfort of the Guide so well as he who has followed close on a wet, fog-shrouded ledge.

48

A BURDEN TO SHARE,
A BURDEN TO BEAR

Bear ye one another's burdens, and so fulfil the law of Christ. For every man shall bear his own burden. *Gal. 6:2, 5*

Paul wrote of a burden to share and a burden to bear, and both relate to a man's struggle for holiness of life as well as effectiveness in service. How many men would have been spared bitter defeat had some brother helped lift a load in a moment of special difficulty when temptation swept in.

An honest word of caution or counsel even at the risk of offending could have spared a fall. Sometimes we need help with the load. We need to learn more perfectly how to cast our cares on the Master Burdenbearer.

We must not hesitate to accept a hand when we find temptation threatening our walk. Ugly pride encrusts the spirit, shutting out sensitivity to potential help from our brothers. No man is so vulnerable as he who refuses to lend a hand to a brother carrying a heavy load across a dangerous passage.

But there is another load, the soldier's pack, and that we must carry alone. Responsibility, temptation, our personalities and eccentricities all cling to our backs and will cling because we still are men. We grow muscles that render the pack acceptable and we make good progress in spite of it.

To learn the difference between the burden to share and the burden to bear lies at the heart of our spiritual maturing.

49

THE ULTIMATE SACRIFICE

Take now thy son, thine only son Isaac, whom thou lovest, and get thee into the land of Moriah; and offer him there for a burnt offering . . . *Gen. 22:2*

There is no record that God ever asked a harder thing of one of His servants. To yield a son to battle has torn many a father's heart, but there was always the hope the son would return. To watch sickness waste the life of a child always leaves that flicker of hope for recovery. But there is no hope in slaying your child with your own hand.

Though God knows the end from the beginning; Abraham didn't. He was prepared to kill Isaac and burn his body on an altar. Don't let the memory of Sunday school pictures, with the ram caught in the thicket, dim your mind to the horrible reality of Abraham's testing. He loved his son, and those of us with children know the depth of that love.

What God does is always exactly right, and He never attempts to justify His actions before man. The complexity of God's working is such that man could not understand anyway. In God's sight there are no tragedies, only circumstances, circumstances that may drive us to Moriah.

In his heart, Abraham had slain his son. God's purpose was fulfilled and Isaac was spared, as was Abraham. But there was another Father and another Son, and neither could spare the other. If you find yourself wondering at God's providence, remember that.

How ambitious we are for our children! Often our ambition is goaded by pride, knowing that a successful child reflects favorable light on the parents. Are we willing to climb Moriah, and yield our children fully to God?

Perhaps the most beautiful thing about the wilderness climb that day was that Isaac asked questions, yet never rebelled. What do you suppose his thoughts were as his father bound him to the altar?

Pray that God will grant such surrender, that Moriah will be possible for you, and that He will grant such trust that your children will walk anywhere you walk with God.

GOD'S BEST GIFT TO MAN

And the Lord God said, It is not good that man should be alone; I will make an help meet for him. *Gen. 2:18*

Why is it some men, including Christians, seem to go out of their way to put down their wives? Do we feel it a mark of weakness to show love for our mates? The man who hurts his wife scorns God's greatest gift.

With due regard for the disciplines of bachelorhood, it seems apparent that man needs a woman to find the fullest meaning in life. God, who designed the creature called man, said, "It is not good that man should be alone." Paul added a profound interpretation to God's statement when he said, "So ought men to love their wives as their own bodies. He that loveth his wife loveth himself" (Eph. 5:28). A wife is a vital, integral part of a husband.

We think badly of a friend who abuses a gift we favor him with. What must God think as He looks down on men today who use cutting humor and boorish manners, who fail to share household tasks, and make selfish decisions regarding money?

Can you imagine Jesus treating His bride, the church, as some men who profess to be Christians treat their wives? With Christ's love as our example, let us continually enrich that person God gave us, His very best gift.